The Kids from
QUILLER'S
BEND

Contents

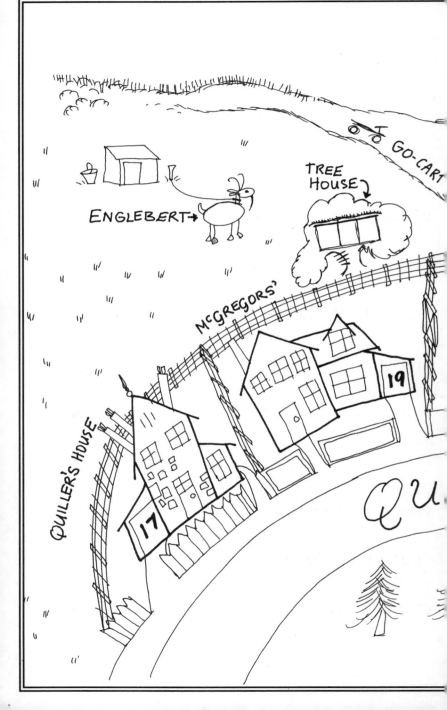

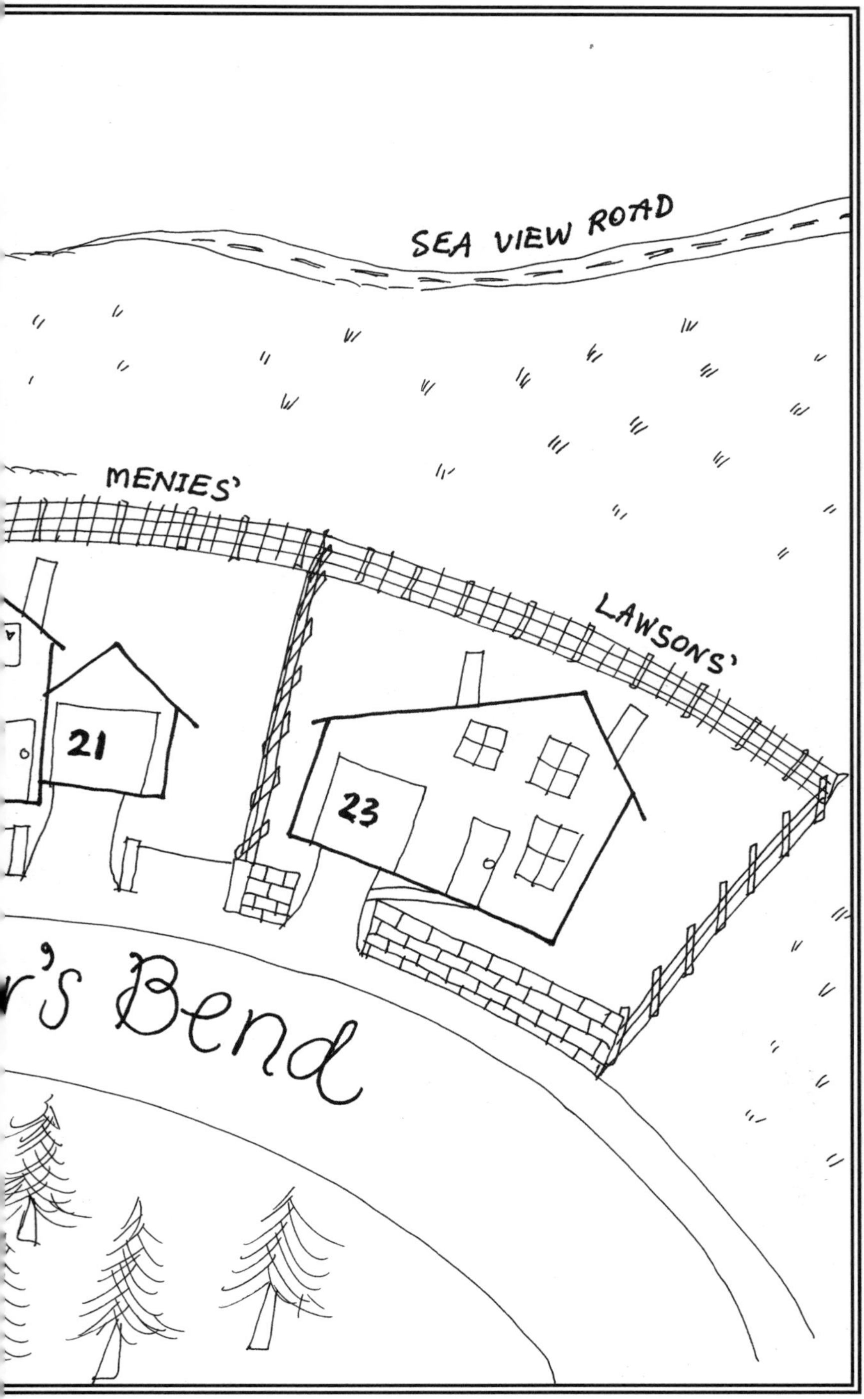
SEA VIEW ROAD
MENIES'
LAWSONS'
21
23
r's Bend

Chapter *1*

Albert Perkins

If you look at a map, you won't find Quiller's Bend. But it is there, halfway up Hill Road. That's why I've drawn my own map of the area. They call it Quiller's Bend because Mr. Quiller was born there in number seventeen. It's a narrow, gray stone house with a high, pointed roof and three tall, skinny chimneys.

All of us kids really like old Mr. Quiller. He waves to us every morning, and gives us treats when we take his mail in to him. He is special to me because he gave me my first china animal – a tiny giraffe. "If you're not allowed to have any real pets," he said, "would you like this instead?" It was the beginning of my collection.

But best of all, it was Mr. Quiller who finally stopped Albert Perkins from hassling us.

The McGregors live next door to the Quiller house in number nineteen. There's eleven-year-old Davy, five-year-old Paula, and their mom and dad.

I'm Sharma Menie, and I'm eleven years old, too. I live in number twenty-one with my four-year-old sister, Jayshree, and my mom and dad. They bought the place when they first got married. They didn't intend to stay, but that was thirteen years ago, and we're still here!

"When we first bought this house, we were going to give it a coat of paint and sell it," Dad told me once. "That was before you came along. Then there was Jayshree, and after that we couldn't afford to move. Anyway, we'd started a garden and..." He shrugged his shoulders. "I don't think we wanted to move."

"You didn't, you mean," Mom said. "There are much nicer parts of town than this. I've always wanted to live up in Brook Terrace."

I shut my mouth tightly, before I said something I shouldn't. We'd have to be crazy to live in Brook Terrace. The Perkins boys live there!

It was ages since Davy and I had had anything to do with Albert Perkins. But we still remembered the day, when we were five years old, that Albert arrived at Baker Street School. That was when we discovered he was a pincher. He pinched everyone he could reach on the mat. One by one, we moved away from him until he was left sitting on his own.

Our teacher, Mrs. Kane, didn't believe Albert was being horrible to us. He sat there innocently, with a tear trickling down each cheek.

"No one will be my friend," he sobbed.

She stepped over us on her stork's legs, stood him up, and led him back to her chair. "Never mind," she said. Then she glared at us through her glasses. "You have been very unkind to poor Albert." She nodded her head at us, her long nose pecking out each word. "And I don't like unkind children."

Albert smirked at us and made sure he didn't wipe away his tears. He turned those same tears on for his mother. Almost every week, she called my mom to tell her how the kids in Quiller's Bend had hit Albert and called him names. She'd wanted to send him to St. Peters, a private school on the other side of town. But Baker Street had been Mr. Perkins's old school, and he wanted his boys to go there.

"We don't hit him. He hits us!" I kept telling Mom. But she didn't believe me. It wasn't fair! Mrs. Perkins believed everything Albert told her, but my mother thought anything I said was a lie.

Albert should have improved as he got older, but he didn't. He got worse. Halfway through his last year at

Baker Street – he was nine then – he was punching, kicking, and hitting with sticks. If his victims dared defend themselves, or even if they didn't, we'd see his mother come to school in her shiny red car. She'd march into the principal's office, dragging Albert's little brother, Richard, behind her. The first time we saw him was scary. Richard was an exact copy of his big brother. He had a round face, soft wavy hair, fat little legs, and an innocent look that was too good to be true.

"Not another one!" Davy whispered behind his hand.

One morning, Mrs. Perkins, Richard, and Albert were in the office with Mr. Atwood for some time. Then Davy and I were called in with the Lawson twins, Marty and Jane. They'd moved into number twenty-three the year before, and we all walked to school together.

You'd never have guessed they were twins. Jane wasn't much taller than I was, and had pale skin and fair hair. She was shy and nervous, always waiting for someone else to tell her what to do. Marty was tall and skinny with bristly black hair. He was the one who always took charge. It was only their eyes, which were dark like melted chocolate, that showed they were brother and sister.

Mrs. Perkins sat by the window. It looked as if her pudgy face had been molded from play-dough, and its narrow lips and arched eyebrows painted on. Crinkly brown hair waved down over her ears and forehead. It almost hid the hard gray eyes that flicked at each of us in turn, finally coming to rest on Marty.

Richard sat on her lap and, every now and then, when the adults weren't looking, he made faces at us. Albert stood beside his mother, leaning on her shoulder. He stared at us, and his eyes seemed to be saying, *I've got you now. This time, all the big guns are on my side.*

Mr. Atwood sat behind his desk. He had a piece of paper in his hand. He laid it flat and looked up at us. "Sharma, Davy, Jane, and Marty." His mouth moved beneath his floppy moustache. "What's all this I've been hearing about you?" Sometimes he sounded fierce when he was really just joking. But this time I couldn't tell, because the sunlight glinted off his glasses and I couldn't see his eyes.

The four of us stared straight ahead, our shoulders touching – except for Marty, who stood one step in front of us. He always went halfway to meet trouble. His hands were behind his back, and I could see his fingers twisting together like a bunch of little snakes.

"Well then, maybe you can tell me which one of you hit Albert Perkins first." I tried to send a message to the others not to say anything. I'd recognized one of Mr. Atwood's traps for catching guilty kids.

They must have gotten the message, because everyone was silent. Then Marty, who'd been out of school last week with a cold, cleared his throat.

"Well, Marty?" Mr. Atwood's eyes swiveled to stare at Marty's face, still splotched with traces of that morning's breakfast. The twins lived with their grandmother, and she didn't always manage to check on things such as clean faces and tidy clothes.

"When, sir?" Marty's voice sounded husky. The snakes grabbed each other and froze.

"When?" Mr. Atwood's eyebrows disappeared into his hair. "Do you mean you've hit him on more than just one occasion?"

Marty rolled his eyes upward till he was gazing at the ceiling. He'd fallen into the trap. If he said no, that meant that he had hit Albert, although not more than once. If he said yes, it meant he'd hit him lots of times.

He was in trouble no matter what he said! Mrs. Perkins and Albert both smirked.

"Marty means, when were we supposed to have hit him?" I interrupted. I'd seen Mr. Atwood doing what he called "getting at the truth" before.

"Oh," he said. "Is that what he means?" I turned red and nodded vigorously. So did the others.

Mrs. Perkins made a snorting noise and looked out the window.

"Well," he leaned forward, "the time I'm talking about is 3:30 p.m. yesterday, on the way home from school." He looked down at his paper. "I've been told that you four hid in old Mr. Quiller's gateway and jumped out at Albert. And," he pointed to the words, "'whacked him with sticks.' What have you got to say about that?" Up went his eyebrows again.

I saw the other three relax. "It wasn't Jane or I, sir," Marty grinned. "Grandma met us after school and took us to the doctor about our coughs. Didn't she, Jane?" He put one hand over his mouth and coughed twice to make sure Mr. Atwood understood.

Jane stared. She didn't say anything. She never said anything. If she tried to speak, only the beginning of the first word came out, over and over again. She had a bad stutter. It was better to leave most of the talking to Marty.

"I didn't do it, either," said Davy. "Mom took me to get new shoes."

"So, that leaves you, Sharma." I thought his mouth twitched a bit as he stared at me. Then he turned to Albert. "Come here, Albert. Take a close look at Sharma." He led Albert around the desk until we stood face to face. Well, not quite face to face. More like my face to his top shirt button. Albert was eight inches taller than I was. I knew that exactly because we'd measured each other the day before. Our teacher had written our heights on the class wall chart. Albert was the tallest student in the room. I was the shortest and also the skinniest.

"Was this the girl who," Mr. Atwood looked down at his piece of paper again, "'whacked you with sticks'? All by herself?"

"Well, how else can you explain the filthy state of his clothes?" Mrs. Perkins demanded. "His teacher said he was spotless when he left school to go home."

"It was the go-cart!" I blurted out.

"That can't be true," Mrs. Perkins insisted. "Albert doesn't have a go-cart."

"The McGregors' go-cart. There was no one home, so he got it out of their shed and took it up the hill."

I saw Albert make his hands into fists. It wouldn't pay to let him catch me on my own after this, but I wasn't stopping now. "He hit the post at the bottom of the path and fell off into the mud." I turned away from Mrs. Perkins. The giggles that had burst out yesterday, when I'd seen Albert fall off the go-cart, were trying to escape again.

"It seems we've solved the mystery of the muddy clothes," Mr. Atwood said.

Mrs. Perkins stood up, took a deep breath, and held onto it like she'd never let it go. She stomped across the floor, pushing Albert in front of her and dragging Richard behind. Mr. Atwood stood up to open the door, but he was too late. She opened it herself, charged out, and banged it shut. The whole room shook. Papers floated to the floor, and we held our breath.

Suddenly, the school bell shrilled through every corner of the building. Without speaking, Mr. Atwood opened the door again, and we filed through.

We worked in silence for the whole morning. It had been a lucky escape.

Chapter 2

Albert Lies Again

It was three months before there were any more complaints from Mrs. Perkins about the way we treated her darling son. We thought he'd been cured of telling lies. We should have known he was getting ready for the big one.

We were sitting outside class before school started when Albert and his mother pulled up in their car and got out. Albert had skinned knees, bruised shins and arms, and a black eye! His mother strode across the playground toward the office. Albert limped behind her. Someone had really beat him up this time.

Jane, Marty, Davy, and I stared at Albert. The same thought whizzed through all our minds. What were we doing yesterday after school? What grown-up could give us an alibi?

The answer to the last question was none. No grown-up had seen us yesterday, because we'd made sure they hadn't! We'd all been together in Grandma Lawson's basement garage while she was having a nap. Looking after nine-year-old twins was hard work when you're nearly seventy, I'd heard her telling Mom.

We weren't supposed to play in Grandma Lawson's garage, because a friend of hers had some things stored there. There was plenty of space alongside the car for the six wooden crates and a stack of cardboard boxes. There was even room left for us to practice the play that we were planning to surprise our parents with during vacation. One of the boxes was full of folded-up curtains and tablecloths. They made fantastic, colorful costumes.

There were velvet cloaks for the two pirates, Davy and Marty. I pinned a pair of silky yellow curtains together over my shoulders and tied the curtain cord around my waist. I was a captured princess. Jane ran on tiptoe around the garage, trailing lace curtains and singing storm songs she made up as she went along. It was funny the way she could sing anything without stuttering, but when she tried to talk, hardly a word came out right. She'd done a high leap into the air, as the pirate ship crashed onto the rocks, and put her foot through the curtain. We had quickly put the curtain back into the box and stopped practicing our play for the day. So, of course, we couldn't say where we'd been.

I'd told Mom I'd been at Davy's. He'd said he was at the Lawsons' – but not in their garage. And the twins said they were at my place. We'd all told lies, and now we were in it up to our necks!

Within five minutes, we were lined up in front of Mr. Atwood's desk – again! This time, I knew he wasn't joking. Anyone could see Albert's injuries were serious. When he asked us where we were yesterday afternoon, we all came out with our separate stories. There'd been no time to decide what we would say!

Albert's story was that we'd been trying to get back at him over the go-cart. That sounded reasonable. We'd been furious when we found out he'd broken one of the axles. Davy's dad had to put on a new one.

"They got me halfway up the shortcut." His voice quivered, and he ended with a sniff. "He," he pointed at Davy, "pushed me down the path, and they," that was Jane and I, "had sticks." More sniffs. "And they hit me here," he touched his bruised arm with one finger and winced, "and here." He pointed to his eye. "And Marty stole my bag." He squeezed out a few tears.

"What did you do with it?" Mr. Atwood asked Marty.

I stared at Mr. Atwood. He believed Albert! Because Marty and Jane wore secondhand clothes, and were often late with money for trips and things like that, we all knew they weren't rich. But they would never steal. How could Mr. Atwood be so stupid?

Marty's face turned red, and then pale. He was angry. "I didn't take it!" The words were forced out one by one. Mr. Atwood's eyes opened wide. He shouldn't have accused Marty of stealing, and he knew it!

Marty leaned on the desk and stuck his neck out. His hair bristled, and his eyes were squeezed into thin slits. "I wouldn't want his rotten bag!"

We were all shocked. No one spoke to Mr. Atwood like that, even if he was wrong. Not even Mrs. Perkins could think of anything to say. Then we heard voices outside. There was a polite knock on the door, and it opened a little. I turned and saw Miss Pitcathley's round face peer through the gap.

"Er, Mr. Atwood?" She blinked several times. Her blue eyes stared at the principal. "There's someone to see you."

Mr. Atwood's eyebrows closed in on each other, making a straight line. "I hope this is important, Miss Pitcathley. You know I'm busy."

"Yes, yes, but..." We heard a restless movement outside, and Miss Pitcathley's head disappeared for a moment. Then she looked in again and went on, "Mr. Quiller is here. It seems he may be able to throw some light on the present problem."

"All right, then. Show him in, and bring another chair." Mr. Atwood sighed. I bet he could see this business going on all morning.

The door swung open, and Mr. Quiller stood there, a tall, bony scarecrow. His wild white hair stuck out like porcupine quills, and eyes like icy blue chips glittered beneath his fuzzy eyebrows. He gazed at each of us, then the papery skin that stretched over his cheeks creased as his mouth widened into a grin. He'd come to save us. I didn't know how, but he was going to fix things. The twisted lump in my stomach disappeared. Jane smiled back at him. Then he turned to Mr. Atwood. Leaning on his cane with one hand, he held up a green canvas backpack in the other.

"I think this belongs to one of you." His voice was like a rasping gate hinge. Mr. Atwood stood and reached out to shake the old man's hand. Mr. Quiller waved him away and dumped the bag on the desk. "I just came to bring the bag. I'll be going now."

"Where did you get it?" Mrs. Perkins demanded, leaning forward from her seat by the window. I glanced at Albert. The look on his face told me his mother shouldn't have asked! But I couldn't have guessed in a hundred years what Mr. Quiller was going to say.

"Do you really want to know?"

"Of course I do!" Mrs. Perkins gave us a spiteful glare. The last time we'd all been here she had ended up looking stupid. Now we were going to pay for it.

Mr. Quiller sat down in the chair Miss Pitcathley had brought in for him. "Well," he said, his bony shoulders hunched under his yellow-and-brown check shirt, "it all started with my Englebert."

Confusion. Davy, Marty, Jane, and I knew Englebert. Albert probably knew of Englebert. But Mr. Atwood and Mrs. Perkins hadn't a clue what Mr. Quiller was talking about.

Mr. Quiller gazed at both of them. He was enjoying himself. "You don't know my Englebert?" he asked. Mr. Atwood shook his head. Mrs. Perkin's eyes narrowed suspiciously.

"Englebert is my goat. He's kept on a long chain fastened to a stake, on the hill behind my house. I move him around from time to time so he can keep the grass cropped. Sometimes this lassie helps me." He reached over and took Jane's hand. She edged across and leaned against him. I'd seen Jane holding Englebert's chain, but I was afraid of him. If we went near, he'd stamp his front feet and stab holes in the air with his horns.

Mr. Quiller patted Jane's hand and smiled. Then he went on, "Englebert is big and black, with a long beard and very sharp horns. And yesterday afternoon..." Mr. Quiller stopped. He looked across at Albert. Albert put his weight on one foot like a sprinter on the starting blocks. Mr. Quiller went on. "Yesterday afternoon, I unhooked this bag from Englebert's horns."

"Where *he* threw it!" Mrs. Perkins stuck out a finger at Marty.

Mr. Quiller shook his head. "Where *he* threw it." He nodded at Albert. "I'd been watching him from my window. First, he threw stones at Englebert. Englebert kept eating. Then the boy got a stick and went closer. When the goat still ignored him, he swung his bag. It hooked around Englebert's horns. Poor Englebert couldn't see where he was going!" Mr. Quiller shook his head again. "In trying to dislodge the bag, he knocked the boy over. I'm afraid Englebert may have jabbed him with his horns. He'll have a few bruises!"

Mr. Atwood stood up. "You four can go," he said to us. He'd seen we weren't far from laughing.

Albert had often teased Englebert. We were glad to see the goat had organized his own justice.

"I'll be going now, too," Mr. Quiller said, and followed us out the door. We walked with him to the gate and watched him drive away in his old car.

"H-How can he f-fit in it? He's got such l-long l-legs," Jane said. That was the most I'd ever heard her say. I looked at her in surprise. I was going to mention it to Marty, but he was looking at the ground with a turned-down mouth and sad eyes. I knew Marty was wondering how Mr. Atwood could have believed that he would steal Albert's bag.

After we left, Mr. Atwood and Mrs. Perkins had a huge argument. We heard the shouting from the playground. But one good thing came of that day. Albert didn't come back to our school. His mother sent him to St. Peters.

Chapter 3

Mr. Quiller

It had been two years since we'd seen Albert Perkins. But we still talked about him every now and then. That's what we were doing today, as we dragged ourselves – in the summer heat – up Hill Road, lugging our bags. They felt as if they were full of bricks. Paula didn't make things any better. She'd just started school and wasn't used to walking all that way.

Now and then, we stopped to rest on someone's fence. It was as though we didn't want to get to Quiller's Bend. Almost as though we knew what was waiting there.

Jane was the first one through the gate at number seventeen. She picked up Mr. Quiller's mail and disappeared with it around the back of the house.

We waited while Queenie, Davy's old black Labrador, padded down the sidewalk to meet us. We all petted her, and she followed us up the walk.

Mr. Quiller was asleep in his chair under the elm tree. Minnie, his cat, was curled up beside him.

Jane bent down and said, "Mr. Quiller?" Her stutter was never very bad when she talked to him. Minnie lifted her head and meowed. But Mr. Quiller didn't answer her.

We were still coming up the walk when Jane stood up and stepped back. Right away, Marty knew something was wrong. He charged across the lawn, legs and arms going everywhere. We chased after him.

Mr. Quiller lay in his chair. His glasses were tilted sideways on the end of his nose, and he looked like a frail bird. Yesterday's newspaper had slid from his lap and made a tent over his feet. A breeze fluttered one of the pages.

Minnie struggled out from under the fingers that lay across her back like a bunch of dry twigs. She purred and bumped her head under my chin when I picked her up. I stared down at the long, bony fingers with their ivory nails. Papery skin covered the blue veins. That was the hand that waved to us out of the car window, that hammered the stake into a new place for Englebert's chain, and that held out a lollipop to Paula when she cried because she didn't want to go to school. That was just last week. And now it wouldn't ever do those things again.

Marty spoke first. "Jane and I'll wait here, Sharma. You go and tell your mom. She'll know what to do."

"I-I w-want to go h-home," Jane quavered.

"You can't go home. You'll upset Grandma." He gently gripped her arm to make sure she didn't take off. "Go on, Sharma. You go, too, Davy. And get Paula out of here." The twins were only a few weeks older than Davy and me, but Marty always took charge when something serious happened.

There weren't many people at the funeral. Mom wasn't sure I should go, but Dad said I could if I wanted. A man in a suit was there. Davy's dad said his name was Mr. Brannigan, and he was Mr. Quiller's lawyer. He was the only person there besides us, the residents of Quiller's Bend.

The twins came in their best clothes. Marty had grown out of his good pants, and I could see the tops of his socks. Jane hung on to Marty's hand as if she'd die if she let go. Her face was worse than pale, it was kind of a yellow color. And if I shut my eyes, I can still see Grandma Lawson's navy blue coat with its fur collar, and her hat with the daisies.

Davy came with his dad. His mom was looking after Jayshree and Paula. It had been decided that they were too young to understand what was going on. They were right about Jayshree. She kept asking me where Mr. Quiller was. And what he had done with the lollipops. He'd promised he would give her one when she started school next year.

When they took the coffin out, I sniffed and hunted for my handkerchief. It was in my pocket, wrapped around the little giraffe Mr. Quiller had given me. I'd grabbed it off the shelf as I'd gone out the door. It had belonged to Mr. Quiller once, and it would want to say good-bye to him. Mom squeezed my hand and said it was all right to cry, so I did. I thought Jane would, too, but she didn't. She just hung on tighter than ever to Marty's hand.

Through the whole service, I sat and thought about how great Mr. Quiller had been to us kids. I couldn't bear for him not to be there when we got home. But as we were driving into Quiller's Bend, I had a thought and said, "But he's not dead, really. He'll never be dead."

"What do you mean?" Dad tried not to run off the road as he looked around at me.

"Because of Quiller's Bend. While it's here, and we're here, and his house is here, especially his house, he'll always be alive." I don't know if Dad agreed with me, but he knew what I meant.

After dinner that night, Jayshree still kept talking about Mr. Quiller. "When's he coming back?" she asked.

"Take her outside to play ball," Mom said. "We'll have to do something to take her mind off it."

On her first throw, Jayshree tossed the ball in the garden. We were looking for it when I heard the gate open. Not the road gate, but the one in the fence between the two houses. Dad and Mr. McGregor had put it in when Davy and I were little. That way, we could go back and forth without having to go out onto the road.

Davy came through first – slowly, backward, and bending over. He was having trouble with something.

"Watch out," he said. "She'll get away."

Then he straightened up, and Paula followed him through. Queenie pushed past them both and stopped in front of Paula. Queenie was wagging her tail and looking up at something Paula held in her arms.

Jayshree was nearest. She raced over to see what it was. "That's Mr. Quiller's cat, Minnie!" she exclaimed. "Put her back. Mr. Quiller will be sad if Minnie isn't there when he comes home."

Davy and I glanced at each other. I shrugged. We'd tried everything to explain what had happened. Mom had insisted we avoid the word "dead." Instead we'd said things such as "gone to sleep" and "gone away." Nothing had worked.

Then Paula looked up from the purring cat, and I was horrified to hear her say, "Mr. Quiller's dead. He's not coming back. So Minnie's mine now." And she grinned like a pirate who had discovered treasure.

Jayshree stared at the cat, then at Paula. She swung around, grabbed my sleeve, and buried her face in my shirt. My little sister never cries quietly. She didn't this time, either. She bellowed so loudly Mrs. McGregor looked out her kitchen window to see what was wrong. Davy signed with both hands to let his mother know not to worry.

Then Queenie barked, and Minnie struggled out of Paula's arms. She sprang through the gate. Queenie panted after her. Paula raced after them both. I saw the cat's tail as she fled under the McGregors' house.

I hugged Jayshree until her crying stopped. She clung to me, her shoulders heaving as she sobbed. Davy raised his eyebrows to ask if she was all right.

I nodded. "At least she understands now," I said. For a second the sobbing increased before dying away again. "But Davy, what's the story about the cat?"

"Mr. Quiller's lawyer..." more sniffles from Jayshree, "was talking to Dad at the funeral. He figured Mr. Quiller knew he didn't have long to go when they met last week. Mr. Quiller was worried about the animals. He asked his lawyer to find someone to look after them. Dad likes cats, so he said we'd take Minnie, but..."

"Englebert!" I said. "What about Englebert?"

"Yeah. That's just it. What about Englebert?"

The sun had gone down, but the long, dry grass behind the houses still shone in the pale light. We scanned the hillside for Englebert and the gray blob that was the corrugated-iron roof of his shelter. There they were, at the top of the hill just below Sea View Road. And although we couldn't see it from our backyard, we knew there'd be a bucket of water beside the shelter.

I counted on my fingers the three days since Mr. Quiller had died. "Someone should have moved

Englebert to fresh grass," I said, "and he'll be needing some more water."

"Yes, but who's going to do it? You know what he's like when we're up there with the go-cart!"

I knew about that all right! We had a good go-cart track that slanted across the hill. It started at the top above number seventeen and finished behind our fence. It was hard work pushing the heavy wooden cart up to the top, but a real thrill when we came whooping down the hill until we rolled off at the bottom. It was always best in the summer, when we could go racing through the tall grass.

But if we went near Englebert, he'd chase us until he was pulled up short by his chain. He never got us, but there was always a chance that he might.

What about Dad? I wondered. Would he move Englebert? No. He didn't like animals. He wouldn't even let us have a pet dog. And we all knew what Mr. McGregor thought about Englebert. We'd heard him say it often enough. There'd never been a goat on that hill when he was a boy!

Jayshree pulled her face away from my shirt and said, "Tell Marty. He'll fix it!" She could be right. Next stop, the Lawsons' house.

It was Jayshree's bedtime, so I pushed her in through the kitchen door. "Mom, here's Jayshree," I called, and ran to catch up with Davy out on the sidewalk. Marty saw us coming, and met us at the gate.

"How's Jane?" I asked.

"Rotten. She won't talk to us. Come in and see if you can do anything with her. I can't."

Jane was in her bedroom with the curtains closed. All I could see in the shadows was a hunched-up shape on the bed and the pale oval of Jane's face.

"Jane," I whispered. "Get up and come downstairs with us." The oval turned away and hid in the pillow.

"Told you," Marty said. Then he went on, "So, what did you come over for?"

Davy told him about Englebert. He finished up by saying, "But you know what he's like. No one can get near him. Remember what a mess he made of Albert Perkins?"

The bed creaked, and Jane sat up. "I-I c-could d-do it." Her voice was rusty with tears, and her stutter worse than ever.

"No, you couldn't," Davy argued. "He'd butt you and pull away. And you'd never be able to move his shelter, or carry that bucket of water up the hill."

32

Jane flopped back onto the pillow. "E-Englebert w-wouldn't b-butt me. H-He l-likes me!"

"He likes her, all right," Marty said. "I've watched her feed him pieces of bread. And she used to hold him while Mr. Quiller moved the stake."

"Could she hold onto Englebert's chain while we moved his stake?" I asked.

"I suppose that might work," Davy agreed slowly. "As long as she didn't let him go."

"A-Are you s-scared, Davy?" Jane was sitting up. I could see a white line of teeth. She was smiling.

"Of course not!" A redness rose up from Davy's neck into his cheeks.

"All right, then," Marty announced. "In the morning. Right after breakfast."

"B-Before breakfast! Englebert w-will be h-hungry."

"OK. Before breakfast. Now, who wants hot chocolate? I'm going to make some."

"M-Me!" Jane scrambled out of bed.

For the next half hour, the four of us sat around the Lawsons' kitchen table, sipping hot chocolate. Davy, Marty, and I were planning how to deal with the goat and where we'd move him. Jane held her mug in both hands. She added nothing. She'd already said more in five minutes than I'd ever heard her say before. As we argued about who had the best idea, her gaze settled on each speaker in turn, and she smiled.

"At least it's given her something else to think about," I said to Davy on the way home.

"I suppose it has. But when we're struggling around the hill with Englebert's shelter and hammering in his stake, and she's wandering around with that fierce beast on the end of a chain – I just hope she knows what she's doing!"

After I got into bed, I began to laugh. I was picturing Englebert chasing Davy around the hill as Jane flew along behind on the end of the chain. The goat would be plunging and rearing like a rocking horse. He'd have his head down and his horns aimed at Davy's fleeing back.

Then I had a horrible thought. What if Englebert chased me? I stopped laughing.

Chapter 4

For Sale

Jane went first. She squeezed between the two top wires of the McGregors' fence. Marty tossed an empty bucket over, and Davy lugged a large hammer. We all squeezed through after her. It had rained in the night, and the grass was damp. It slipped under our feet as we scrambled up the hill.

"I'm glad Jane remembered the water tap by the road," Marty said when we were about halfway up. "I wouldn't want to cart this all the way if it was full!"

But Davy had put his hammer down and was gazing uphill. "Englebert could just about get us from here," he said. He glanced from the nearest fence, to the goat, and back to the fence. "I'm not going any farther."

Jane turned around and snickered at him. Davy blushed. "Well, he could so get us from here – nearly."

The goat had eaten a large circle bare of grass. Now he was pulling at the end of his chain to reach a leafy blade that had leaned over into his territory. Jane was right. He was hungry. She bent down and pulled out a handful of grass. After a few more steps up the hill she stopped, held out the grass, and called softly, "E-Englebert, c-come here."

The chain rattled as Englebert lifted his head and stared at us. He was chewing on a stalk. Each time his jaw moved, his long beard flicked to the side.

"E-Englebert," Jane called again. The goat shook his head. The morning sun gleamed on the tips of his horns. Jane rustled the handful of grass and climbed a few feet farther up the hill. Now she was inside Englebert's circle. We weren't. Our feet were still hidden in the long grass, where his chain wouldn't let him reach us.

Stepping high on his neat, black hooves, the goat came down the hill.

"Be careful, Jane," Marty whispered. He was watching those horns.

But I was staring at Englebert's eyes. They were strange eyes, pale gold, with a dark streak across the center. They looked blind, yet I knew he could see us.

He stopped too far away for Jane to grab the leather collar that was hanging loose around his scrawny neck.

But he was near enough to stretch out and nibble at the grass she offered. She leaned toward him. One gentle hand caressed his velvety ear. He tossed his head, but his feet didn't move. He took another mouthful, and she stroked him again.

Jane stopped stroking and slid her hand down his neck. She slipped her fingers inside his collar. With her spare hand, she waved us toward the stake.

Who was going first? We looked at each other. I'm not very good with animals, so I was surprised to find myself leading the way. The plan was that we should move the stake first. Then, while Englebert was busy with the fresh grass, he wouldn't notice us messing around with his shelter and water bucket.

The chain was attached to a ring near the top of the stake. The trouble was that Englebert, in trying to reach the last of the grass, had pulled it so tight I couldn't undo the catch.

"Give me a hand," I yelled to the boys. They'd come farther up the hill, but were still outside the circle. They took a few reluctant steps toward me, but then I felt the chain go slack. "Never mind." I bent down and had the catch undone in a second.

"Look out!"

I spun around. The goat was charging uphill with Jane hanging onto his chain. As I'd pictured the night before, he was plunging and rearing – at me!

I scrambled for the long grass beyond the edge of the circle. But even before I reached it, I realized it wouldn't help. Now that I'd undone the chain, Englebert could go anywhere.

Jane was like a ship's anchor in a storm. By digging in her heels, she slowed Englebert down, but she couldn't stop him. Remembering that I'd once heard someone say, "There's safety in numbers," I headed for the two boys, but they were already flying down the hill. I used to think Marty would do anything to help his sister, but now he was just trying to save himself!

Davy and Marty were already safe on the other side of the fence when I slid on a muddy patch. I rolled a couple of times before thumping into a hollow. When I stopped, I was facing uphill. Englebert, with his needle-sharp, pointed horns and his slanting eyes, skidded to a halt no more than a yard away.

He shook his head, rattling his chain and flicking his beard. He took a couple of more steps. As he tilted his horns toward me, I cringed into the hollow and shut my eyes.

How long did I lie there? I don't remember. The wet grass must have been cold on my bare legs, but I didn't feel it. Birds were chirping in our fruit trees, but I scarcely heard them. I was too busy listening to the sound of Englebert puffing and snorting in my ear.

Then there was a tug at my sleeve, and someone giggled. Hot air huffed into my hair. A moist nose nuzzled my neck. I slid my arm to the side and opened one eye. Yellow teeth tugged at my sleeve again, and there was more giggling.

"C-Come on, Englebert." Jane was laughing as she heaved on the chain. "D-Don't b-be scared, Sharma," she said. "Englebert l-likes g-girls."

He was quiet now, and she led him down to the old oak tree near the McGregors' fence. She fastened his chain around it while the boys moved the stake. Then they found a good place for his shelter while we filled his bucket.

Jane was right about Englebert liking girls. He certainly didn't like boys! Maybe Albert had soured him. After that, Jane and I walked him to fresh grass every second day, and left the other jobs to the boys!

The notice appeared ten days after Mr. Quiller's funeral. Davy and I were up in our tree house trying to escape from our pesky little sisters. The tree house was in the old oak tree that grew on Mr. Quiller's side of the back fence. Most of the branches hung over the McGregors' side, so Davy considered it his.

Parts of the tree house were ancient. A platform had been built a long time ago. Now the branches had grown around it so it was part of the tree. We'd nailed wood around the platform for walls. Then we found a carpet at the dump. Mom was mad when Mr. McGregor let us bring it home. "What a horrible, filthy thing," she'd said. But it made a good roof when we slung it between two branches.

We'd been lying on our stomachs that afternoon, drinking lemonade and eating gingersnaps. I was dropping pieces of cookie down onto the ground. Old Queenie was sitting under the tree, wagging her tail and waiting for them.

"Who do you think that is?" Davy stood up to get a better look at the car that'd pulled up at Mr. Quiller's gate. I stopped feeding Queenie and stood up, too.

A woman wearing a black skirt and jacket and high heels got out. As she turned around to open the back door, I saw her well-styled hair. Davy was quite right to ask who she was. We didn't see many people as well dressed as that around here.

She dragged something out of the backseat, lugged it across the sidewalk, and leaned it against the fence. It was a sign. Then she got out a hammer. She bashed away at the sign until it stood more or less straight. When she stepped back to admire her work, we could see what was written on the sign: "For Sale."

After she'd gone, we went down to take a closer look. The name and phone number of the real-estate agent were printed underneath.

I thought I'd gotten over being sad about Mr. Quiller, but I rubbed my eyes and sniffed as we looked over his gate. The windows reflected only shadows from the elm tree. And with no smoke drifting up from the kitchen chimney, the house looked dead. Already the lawn had grown, and the edges looked ragged. Mr. Quiller hadn't bothered much with a flower garden, but he always grew vegetables. And now there were weeds coming up between the rows of carrots and spinach.

"Come on. We can't hang around here all day." Davy's voice was loud, but I knew he didn't feel any better than I did. We tried to cheer ourselves up by guessing who would buy the house. Davy hoped it'd be a family with some boys. "There's too many girls here already," he said.

But weeks went by, and the For Sale sign faded and tilted to one side. Only four groups of people came to look at the house. The real-estate agent kept a smile on her face while she pointed out the "wonderful view" and the "valuable extra land behind the house." But she didn't make a sale.

By July, the lawn was as long as the grass on Englebert's hill. Marty suggested moving the goat onto the property to crop it down. But it had been a good growing season, and he had all he could manage on the hill. He'd grown fit and livelier than ever, and his coat was long and silky. He still wouldn't let the boys come near. But when Jane and I climbed the fence, he'd step daintily up to us to see what we had brought him. Sometimes it was only grass, but more often it was crusts of bread, or goodies from the cookie jar.

One day, we watched the real-estate agent come by. She used the hammer to whack the sign from side to side until it flopped over onto the ground. She rummaged around for a cloth, wiped the dirt off the sign, and piled everything into the trunk of her car. She dusted her hands against each other and drove away.

"She's given up," Marty announced, and suggested we should take the go-cart up the hill to celebrate. The boys hadn't been excited about riding the go-cart lately. But this morning, we'd moved Englebert to the far side of the hill.

Jane and I sat on the edge of Sea View Road and watched Marty and Davy race down the track, faster and faster, over bumps and through dips. Their whoops and yells were swept straight back by the wind. So was Davy's hair. But Marty's was too short, it still stuck up like a scrub brush.

When they got near the bottom, we knew it wasn't hard for them to swing their weight and steer off to one side before they hit the fence post. It just looked impossible. That's why we were holding our breath, and didn't hear the purring engine noise until the long white car stopped behind us on the road.

Chapter 5

Richard Perkins

I don't know why we ducked down behind the bushes. Mr. Quiller's lawyer knew we were looking after Englebert, and he'd said we could go on using the land just the way we always had. But I felt nervous, and Jane looked frightened.

After a few minutes, the car started to move off slowly. It rumbled a few yards along the road then stopped again. Jane and I peered through the bushes. Faces stared out through the tinted glass of the side windows. What were they looking at, and who were they? One back window opened and an arm came out. A hand waved toward the far end of the hill.

"Wh-What are they l-looking at?" Jane whispered.

I turned so my gaze could follow the pointing hand. That part of the hill was empty – except for Englebert. He'd been grazing on the fresh grass we'd moved him to that morning. Now he stopped and faced the road.

He stamped one front foot, shook his head, and marched uphill toward the car.

The car started up again. This time it kept going, but still very slowly. We stood up to watch. As it reached the corner, two heads stuck out of the back window. I recognized the Perkins boys. One of them waved and the other poked out his tongue. Then the car disappeared.

"What were they doing here?" Davy asked when I told him who I'd seen. The two boys had pushed the go-cart up so we could have our turn.

"I don't know."

"Sharma, didn't you ask?"

"Not with their mother there."

"You're not scared of her, are you?"

"I won't have anything to do with them," I said.

Marty's eyebrows made a heavy ridge over his eyes. He'd never forgotten or forgiven Albert for saying that he'd stolen his bag. Marty's funny like that. His friends, that's us, could do anything, and he wouldn't be upset. But Albert – he'd lied about Marty, and Mr. Atwood had believed him. And in the fuss that followed, Mr. Atwood had never set things straight. He hadn't even said he was sorry.

So it was just as well that Marty and Jane had to go to town with their grandmother after school the next day, because when Davy, Paula, and I got home, the long white car with dark windows was parked in our driveway. The Perkinses. Two days in a row!

"I'm coming over to your place," I said to Davy.

"Don't be stupid. Find out what's going on, then come over and tell me."

"You come with me."

"Well... I... I've got homework to do."

"You're not scared of their mother, are you?" Remembering what he'd said yesterday, I smirked at him. One point for me!

My mother was serving coffee in the living room, not in the kitchen where she and Dad usually had it. Mrs. Perkins sat on the sofa, and one of our best cups and saucers sat on a small table beside her. There was a half-eaten cream cake on a plate on her lap. She picked it up and took a bite. Cream stuck to her top lip. I drooled. Those cakes came from Jackson's Bakery. They were my favorites. Maybe having Mrs. Perkins over wasn't such a bad idea!

"Say good afternoon to Mrs. Perkins, Sharma." Mom was using her "lady's voice."

"Good afternoon, Mrs. Perkins." The sooner I got the polite part out of the way, the sooner I'd get a cake. There was still one left on the plate. I reached for it.

"For goodness sake, Sharma, remember your manners. You're behaving as though you've never been taught any. Offer the plate to the guests first."

There was a movement behind me. If I hadn't been concentrating on the cake, I'd have seen Albert and Richard when I first came in. They were sitting on the window seat. Richard was licking cream off his fingers and turning the pages of Dad's stamp album. Dad would have gone crazy if he'd seen Richard looking at the album and eating at the same time.

I thought I knew what would happen when I held the plate out to Albert. But I was wrong. He said, "No thanks, Sharma. I've already had one." He hadn't forgotten his manners! But Richard burped and took it. I watched the cherry on the top disappear into his wide-open mouth.

"Never mind, dear," Mom said. "You can make yourself a sandwich."

I scowled at the empty plate and carried it out to the kitchen. There was a tomato in the fridge. I sliced it and put it between two pieces of bread. Then I sneaked outside. I wasn't going to have that greedy little pig smirking at me eating a sandwich while he swallowed the last of the cake.

Jayshree would be next door. She always shot over there as soon as Paula got home from school. Jayshree looked up to Paula, who was five. With a bit of luck, Davy would be somewhere around, too. We could hide in the tree house until the Perkins boys went home. They'd never see us from our place.

We sat up in the tree house and dug up all the complaints we had about the Perkins boys. Then suddenly, something whacked into the trunk of the tree, causing the leaves to shiver. We looked over the side. It was Albert and Richard.

"Bet that gave you a fright!" Albert shouted up at us. "Thought we were still inside, didn't you?"

I had thought they were still inside. But they must have come out, gotten through the fence, and sneaked up the hill. They'd have seen us from there. And now they had a piece of lumber, and were using it like a battering ram against the tree.

49

"Hey, cut that out. You'll damage the tree!" Davy yelled angrily.

"It's not your tree!" Richard tilted his head back. He still had cream around his mouth.

"Who said?"

"My mom said!"

"What does she know?"

"My mom said..." Richard didn't say any more, because Albert jabbed him in the ribs with his elbow.

"Shut up," Albert muttered in his brother's ear. "Dad said not to tell." He grabbed his brother's arm and dragged him along the fence line. Then Albert climbed through between the top two wires, but Richard obviously hadn't finished smashing things. He clambered onto the fence and began to swing his body back and forth. The wires screeched and the fence posts swayed.

"Get off there!" I yelled. "You'll wreck the fence!" It was my turn now. It was our fence he was wrecking. I slithered down the ladder and raced across the McGregors' lawn. As I ran through the gate, I was still yelling. I didn't run out of breath until I stood panting in front of the seven-year-old monster who had almost torn out two of our fence posts.

"It's not your fence!" he sneered.

"Of course it's our fence," I panted, grabbing the wires to hold him still.

"It's not!" He wrenched free.

"Whose do you think it is then, stupid?" I was so mad, I shoved him hard. It took him by surprise, and he tipped over backward, landing on his back. He yelped and began to cry.

All this time, Albert had stood back, saying nothing. If I'd thought about it, I'd have been surprised. From what I remembered, it wasn't like Albert not to join in a fight. Even now, all he said to me was, "Now you've done it!" And he crawled through the fence and stood his young brother up on his feet.

Richard stopped crying. His eyes had been squeezed shut with sobbing. But now they opened wide. They were round and gray, and swamped with tears. "It's half ours, this fence," he bawled. "That's ours, too!" He waved his arm at the hillside. "That tree's ours, and Mom said we can cut it down if we want!"

"Shut up, Richard!" Albert shook his brother's arm, but there was no stopping him.

"And that goat. He's going to be ours, too, and we can do whatever we like with him. Mom said he's a nasty beast!"

"Don't tell lies!" Davy joined in the fight, but he didn't sound too sure. He'd turned pale. One hand reached out for the fence and held on like a claw. Richard seemed very sure of himself.

I looked at Albert. "Is that true?"

Albert nodded. "Dad made an offer for the land this morning. He said no one else was interested in it. They'll snap the offer up." So that was why Mrs. Perkins had come visiting – to spread the good news!

"Are you going to live in Mr. Quiller's house?" I asked. I couldn't think of anything worse than having the Perkinses living in Quiller's Bend.

But there was something worse. And Albert began to tell us about it.

"We wouldn't live in that old dump!" he said. The sneering voice we hadn't heard for a couple of years was back. "Dad's going to bulldoze it down and put condominiums there. He might build for us farther up the hill. Mom says she likes the view. Then he'll divide the rest of the land up for more building sites."

So that's what they were doing yesterday, checking out the land. Jane and I hadn't felt good about seeing them there, but we never could have guessed it was as bad as this. I stared across at number seventeen. In a way, I was looking at it for the first time. It was different from all the other houses on Quiller's Bend, with its gray stone walls; the afternoon sun reflecting off its long, narrow windows; the slate roof with its two little attics; the chimneys like pointing fingers; and the front door, painted dark green with a carved knob set right in the middle.

I remembered Mr. Quiller sitting in his chair in the back garden, reading the paper we'd brought in for him. Or maybe he'd have gone inside by now and made a cup of coffee in the kitchen, which hadn't been changed since the house was built. That was more than a hundred years ago. How silly we were to have been fussing over who might live there. Anyone would have done. Anyone would have been better than this.

Now the house would be crushed under the bulldozer's blade. There'd be nothing left for us to remember. Mr. Quiller would really be gone then.

Davy and I went back through the gate and sat on his porch. "Can they do that?" I asked.

"I don't see why not." Davy poked at a patch of moss growing on the shady side of the step. Then he stood up and walked slowly around the side of the house. Queenie followed him. Her head hung down, and so did her tail. She knew things were bad.

When Davy didn't come back, I went to look for him. He was standing under the tree house.

"I can't believe they'd cut it down," I said. I leaned over the fence and patted the lumpy bark.

"I don't know what Dad'll say. And Paula. I caught her trying to climb the ladder the other day."

"Maybe they won't do it."

"I figure that'll be the first thing Mrs. Perkins will do! Just to get back at us. Remember the time we had all that fuss over Albert saying we beat him up?"

"But we didn't do it!"

"That made it worse. Mrs. Perkins ended up looking stupid. She hated it! And she hates us!"

Just then, the Lawsons' car pulled into their driveway. I thought about going to tell them the horrible news. But Marty and Jane would be helping their grandma bring in the groceries. Anyway, I didn't want to see Jane's face when she heard about the house and the land. It would take her only two seconds to figure out that it meant trouble for Englebert, too.

"I'm going inside." Davy wandered down the path, kicking at a stone. Watching him walk slowly away, I could see how miserable he felt. Queenie plodded after him. There was nothing left for me to do but go home. I was going to take Jayshree with me, but she was playing in the sandbox with Paula. It probably would have started a big fight, and I'd had enough of that for one day.

Mrs. Perkins's car was still in the driveway. I saw a head sticking up in the backseat. It was one of the boys, but I couldn't tell which one. I went on across the lawn to the back door. I heard Mrs. Perkins's voice as soon as I opened the door.

"And it's a wonderful school, Mrs. Menie. Simply wonderful! All the children have such beautiful manners. There's none of this fighting and rough behavior you see so much of these days. And of course there's..."

Crash!

I stood still with one hand on the doorknob. That noise came from my room. Who was in there? I kept the door shut because of Jayshree. She was always wanting to play with my little animals. They were so fragile, I let her touch them only if I was there, too.

I dropped my bag and raced up the stairs. I met Richard Perkins, who was taking two steps at a time on his way down. In his haste, he stumbled into me. After I made sure I hadn't broken any bones, I limped into my bedroom.

The display shelf Dad had made for me was hanging from one hook, and all of my precious little animals were scattered across the floor. At my feet was a tiny gray-and-black elephant – without its trunk. I knelt down and picked it up.

As if that rotten kid hadn't done enough to make me miserable, now he'd done this!

Sniffling back the tears that had been threatening for the last hour, I spread newspaper on the floor. Then I started picking up the pieces. A lion with one ear missing. The giraffe. Mr. Quiller's giraffe. I turned it over and examined it. A miracle. It was still in one piece — even its long, slender neck hadn't broken. I found two Dalmatian puppies, but the third was scattered over the floor in tiny pieces! And where was the little rooster? It had such a bright red comb. Even if it had been in a hundred pieces, I should have found some of them.

Some of the animals, such as the giraffe, had been presents. Some I'd bought with birthday money. Others I'd bought when we'd been on vacation. All of them were special. Now, most of them were smashed.

Spots of blood appeared on my fingers where they'd been jabbed by the sharp broken pieces. I was staring at my hands when someone touched my shoulder. I turned and looked into Jayshree's horrified eyes. "Sharma," she whispered. "Your animals!"

We hugged each other, both of us crying – Jayshree for me, and me for everything that had happened that afternoon.

"Sharma! Are you up there?" Mom's footsteps were on the stairs as Mrs. Perkins was backing down the drive. "Did you have to upset the Perkins boys while they were here with their mother?" She stood at the top of the staircase.

"Goodness me!" For a moment she looked as upset as I felt. Then her expression changed to impatience. "But you shouldn't have pushed him. You've only got yourself to blame."

"What did Richard say?" I stood up. I had a feeling of being in this situation before – years ago.

"Just what happened. That you were angry because he was in your room. You tried to push him out, and he crashed into the shelf."

"Do you believe him?"

"Well, you know you make a dreadful fuss if Jayshree's in here on her own."

I couldn't argue anymore. In just two steps I was on my bed with my face buried in the pillow and my hands over my ears. I didn't want to hear any more.

Chapter 6

Bulldozers at Quiller's Bend?

It was Saturday morning, and I didn't want to get up. There wasn't anything to get up for. The tree outside my window was being lashed around by the wind, and gray clouds blanketed the sky. It was going to rain.

Last night, Dad had screwed the display shelf onto the wall again, and I'd put the little animals back. That is, the ones that were left. But when I looked across the room, all I could see were the gaps. Dad said he'd get me more to take the place of the broken ones, but it wouldn't be the same. I pulled the covers up around my ears and shut my eyes.

"Sharma?" It was Jayshree.

"Go away."

"But Jane and Marty are here."

"That's right. We've got to move Englebert." I pulled on my old jeans and T-shirt and went downstairs with my shoelaces flapping.

"For goodness' sake, tie your shoes, Sharma," Mom said. "You don't want people to see you looking like a scarecrow!"

Last night, Mom had finally agreed that Richard was to blame for all the damage, and that it might be a good idea to make sure he didn't get into my room again, even if it did offend Mrs. Perkins. But here she was again, worrying about what other people might think.

"And what about your breakfast?" she called as we went out the door.

"I don't want it."

"But I've made your toast!"

"I'll take it." Marty grabbed the toast off the plate and took a big bite. He was always hungry. Mom frowned. She didn't like pushy children – unless their mother was the president of the Garden Club!

Jane and I set off up the hill while Marty went to get Davy. The wind whipped the grass around our legs and our hair across our faces.

"I l-love the w-wind!" Jane shouted.

"I hate it!" That wasn't true. But I felt rotten, knowing what I had to tell Jane about Englebert and the Perkinses.

"Wh-What's wrong?" She grabbed my arm. But before I had time to answer, she saw something up on Sea View Road. It was a truck with a builder's shed on the back. The long arm of a crane stuck out one side.

The truck crept along to a place where the land below the road was almost flat. Two men got out and unloaded lumber onto the roadside. The wind was much stronger up there. It tugged at their clothes. One man had to chase after his hat and stamp on it with one foot before it escaped altogether.

"Wh-What are they doing?"

"Forget about them. Let's get Englebert before the boys come." I dragged at Jane's sleeve, but she pulled away from me.

By now, one of the men was back in the driver's seat. The other climbed onto the back of the truck and stood there, his hands on his hips, and his hat jammed down tightly over his ears. The crane swung around, and the man hooked it onto the roof of the shed. Then he jumped down and stood back.

The shed rose off the truck and swayed over to the right. Then, as the crane slowly lowered the shed, a gust of wind caught the shed and swung it back against the truck. We heard the bang even over the sound of the wind. It took several minutes, and a lot of shouting, before the shed was safe on the ground and the men could put in stakes to brace it.

Davy and Marty were on their way by this time, so I managed to persuade Jane to get on with the job of moving Englebert. Half an hour later, he was eating fresh grass, and his shelter was protecting him from the worst of the wind.

"I-I'm going to s-see what they're d-doing now," Jane insisted when we'd finished, and she marched off up the hill. She had a head start on me, and on the boys. When we got there, one man was already answering her first question.

"It's a builder's shed," he was saying as he shut the door and pushed the bolt across.

"Wh-What builder?"

The other man lifted a sign off the truck and hooked it onto the shed. "He's the boss," he announced. And we read the sign: "Perkins – Builder."

"Which Perkins?" Marty wanted to know.

"That one," the man nodded toward the white car that cruised to a stop behind the truck. Albert, Richard, and a man who must have been their father climbed out. I'd never seen Mr. Perkins before. And the man

63

didn't look much like the boys. In fact, he looked quite nice, but it had to be him.

"Any trouble?" he said to the men.

"Not much. Just the wind."

"Yes, it's a little rough, all right." Mr. Perkins faced into the wind that howled up from the sea. "I don't know how my wife's garden will like it."

Then he saw us. "Hi, kids," he said. "Been watching what's going on? There'll be more to see in a few days. All kids like watching the bulldozer at work." He gave us a friendly smile before turning to check on the shed.

Didn't he know that Quiller's Bend was the last place on earth we'd want to see a bulldozer? Now that we knew Richard wasn't lying, we'd have to tell Marty and Jane everything. But we didn't get a chance. Richard did it for us. Behind his father's back, he stuck out his tongue. Then he came up close and repeated yesterday's story about what would happen to Mr. Quiller's house, our tree house, and worst of all, Englebert. Albert kept out of it. He leaned against the car and avoided looking at us. He had one hand in his pocket and was fidgeting with something.

Jane was the first to turn away. I could see she was upset as she stomped down the hill. She was huddled in the shelter of the oak tree when I caught up with her. Mr. Perkins might have smiled and acted friendly, but I was mad at him and his kids. Quiller's Bend had gotten along just fine without them. How dare he come along and wreck everything!

I put both my arms around Jane's shoulders. Tears glued her fair hair to her cheeks. I wanted to tell her it would be all right. But I couldn't, because it wouldn't! It wouldn't ever be all right again! She tried to say something to me, but her stutter was so bad no real words came out. It was all the Perkinses' fault! I glared back over my shoulder. Where were they?

The white car had gone, and the truck was pulling out. Marty and Davy stood on the roadside talking to someone. It had to be Albert. After a minute, Marty flung his arms into the air and stormed down the hill. Davy ran to catch up with him. They were stopping and starting all the way. I could see they were arguing. Albert was walking behind them. What did he want?

"He wants to talk to you," Davy told me.

"I told him not to bother!" Marty muttered. "We don't want to hear anything he's got to say." His face was so white his eyes looked like black pebbles in the snow. I'd never seen him so angry. He grabbed his sister's arm. "Come on, Jane. Let's get out of here. It looks like he's coming down anyway!"

Jane stumbled along behind him. I didn't know whether to run after them or wait and listen to Albert.

"What does he want?" Davy demanded.

"How on earth would I know? I don't even know if I want to find out. Not after what happened yesterday!"

Then I told him all about Richard and my broken china animals.

"He what?" Davy looked shocked.

"He pulled them off the wall and smashed half of them."

"And you're going to stand around here chatting with his brother?"

I stared at Albert. He was still coming. He was about halfway down by now. It would serve him right if I waited till he was almost here and then walked off! But something about the determined way he'd stood up to Marty made me think again. Anyway, I was curious.

"Maybe it won't do any harm to listen," I said.

"Well, you can listen by yourself. I don't want to hear any of it." Using the bottom rung of the tree house ladder as a step, Davy climbed over the fence. He marched into his house and slammed the door. I turned and waited for Albert.

"This is yours, isn't it?" He was about two feet away when he took his hand out of his pocket and unwrapped something from his handkerchief. He held it out to me. It was my little china rooster with the red comb.

Chapter 7

Albert Apologizes

I tried to keep my hand from shaking as I took the little bird. "Did Richard give this to you?"

Albert's mouth made a straight line, as if he was trying to smile, but couldn't quite manage it. "Not exactly. I took it from him in the car. He said you gave it to him."

"He's lying! He stole it. And he also smashed a lot of the others."

"What's this about Richard smashing the others? What others?"

"Didn't he tell you about them? About the elephant and the puppy and... I can't remember what else!"

Albert frowned. "I suppose that's what Mom was busy scolding him about last night before Dad came home."

"She must have known about it. You could have heard the crash from out here."

68

"She'd have known, all right. But she wouldn't do anything. She thinks if she pretends these things don't happen, then no one will know what a rotten kid he is. And that makes him worse. He thinks he can get away with anything!"

While he was talking, I was remembering the last afternoon we were all in Mr. Atwood's office, and Mrs. Perkins had repeated Albert's lies about us beating him up, and Marty stealing his bag.

"You should know all about lying," I blurted out. I must have sounded spiteful.

By the embarrassed look on Albert's face, he'd remembered, too. He swung his shoulders as he shifted his weight from one foot to the other. "That was a long time ago. I thought you'd have forgotten."

"Marty hasn't. He's never felt good about Mr. Atwood thinking he stole your bag. And you never did anything to make it right."

Albert clenched his fists at his sides and stared at the ground. He looked lonely. For a moment, I felt sorry for him. Then I jolted myself back to the real world. What was I doing feeling sorry for Albert Perkins? The others would kill me if they knew!

I turned around, climbed through the fence, and ran. I didn't look back until I got to our kitchen door. Albert was standing in the place where I'd left him. He looked miserable, and I didn't care.

I was putting the little rooster in its place on the shelf when I remembered Albert's father had already gone. Albert would have to walk home! Rain streaked the windows and tapped on the roof. For the second time, I almost felt sorry for him. But not quite.

The rain kept up the rest of Saturday and all day Sunday. It was really depressing. Englebert wasn't enjoying it, either. He was hunched up inside his shelter, with only his head poking through the doorway.

After lunch, I sorted through the broken pieces of china for the third time. But I couldn't find enough pieces of anything to be able to stick them together.

Disgusted, I sat on my bed, staring out the window at Mr. Quiller's house. The gray stone walls were dark with rain. Water spurted from one corner of the roof where the gutter needed fixing. It was depressing.

Then someone pounded on our back door. It had to be Davy. No one else made that kind of noise. I quickly ran downstairs.

"Let's go over to Marty and Jane's," Davy suggested. He stood on the step, water dripping off his jacket.

"Wait here, I'll just go and tell Mom where we're going," I said, grabbing my coat off the hook and putting it over my head. A few minutes later, we were racing through the rain, jumping over puddles on the sidewalk.

"We're back to square one," Marty said when he opened the door. "Jane's in bed, she's been crying, and she won't talk to anyone."

"Is it about Englebert?"

"Yeah. Richard Perkins said they'll get rid of him. You can guess what that means. Anyway, you'd better come in."

We hung our wet coats in the kitchen and followed Marty through the house. The air felt damp and cold. The awful weather made the house seem dark and depressing.

Grandma Lawson was having her afternoon nap, so we tiptoed upstairs. It was like a rerun of the day after Mr. Quiller's funeral. Jane was huddled under the bedspread, and this time, there was no way we could entice her out. We stood by the door, whispering as though someone were ill. In a way, Jane was.

I felt we were traitors, leaving Marty to deal with her on his own, but ten minutes later, Davy and I were splashing through the rain to his place. We played cards until dinnertime. I lost most of the games, as I couldn't concentrate. I was worried about Jane. As soon as we got one thing right for her, something else went wrong. She was as delicate as my china animals.

On Monday morning, the rain had gone. So had the clouds. This was the last week of school before vacation, and we'd all been looking forward to it. There wouldn't be much school work. We'd spend most of our time practicing for the school concert and playing sports. But after seeing Mr. Perkins arrive with his builder's shed on Saturday, we felt as rotten as if it were a test day.

Worst of all, Jane didn't come to school.

"What's wrong with her?" I asked Marty when he came out of their gate alone.

Marty shrugged. "Nothing we've really got a name for – unless you want to call it 'the blues.'"

"Is she still in bed?"

"She was when I left."

"What did your grandma say?"

"A lot! But it didn't make any difference. Jane can be stubborn when she wants to!"

Later that morning, Miss Pitcathley called me to the office to ask me to run an errand for her. As I shut the office door, I saw Albert Perkins putting his bike into the bike stand.

Albert Perkins! Putting his bike into our bike stand! What was he up to? I was about to go over and find out when Miss Pitcathley leaned out the window. "Hurry up, Sharma," she chirped. So I had to run. I didn't see him after that. Any other time, I'd have told the boys. But we were all too miserable today, especially Marty. Talking about Albert Perkins would have only made it worse!

The morning dragged on and on. Finally, it was almost lunchtime. We were painting and decorating story cards when Mr. Atwood called over the intercom for Marty to come to the office.

"What's he done, now?" one of the girls whispered to me. Marty went white, like he does when he's nervous – or angry. He stood up, washed the green paint off his hands at the sink, and went out the door. It shut with a thud. Any louder and he'd have been called back for slamming it!

I didn't get much painting done. I kept thinking about Albert Perkins, and wondering if he had anything to do with Marty being called to the office. Was Marty in trouble? Or did it have to do with Jane? What if there was something wrong with Grandma Lawson? I'd often wondered who'd look after the twins if something happened to her.

Marty still hadn't come back when the bell rang for lunch. Davy and I found him in the coatroom, sitting on the seat by his peg. He was holding an envelope.

I was trying to think of a tactful way to ask what was going on. But Davy dived straight in. "What did he want?" he demanded.

Marty looked up. "You'd never guess." He handed the envelope to Davy. "Look at this."

Davy took out a piece of paper. I watched his lips move as he read. When he'd finished, his eyebrows arched, and he handed the paper back to Marty.

"What's it about?" I poked Davy's arm.

"It's from Albert Perkins," Marty said. "He's apologizing for telling lies about us, especially for saying that I took his bag."

"Why would he want to do that?" Davy was confused. "He sure waited long enough, didn't he?"

"Maybe he just realized how bad we all felt about it." I was thinking back to yesterday. Was Albert trying to make things right?

"And that's not all," Marty went on. "Mr. Atwood said he hoped I hadn't thought he believed Albert's lies, and he was sorry if he'd in any way given me that impression."

"Mr. Atwood! Apologizing?" Davy couldn't believe it.

"That's what it sounded like."

"It must be the first time ever!"

"Hey, you two!" I interrupted them. I wasn't going to have them insulting Mr. Atwood. "He's really not that bad!"

"Well, no. I suppose he isn't." Marty tucked the letter into his pocket. "Come on. Let's go eat." As he dragged his lunchbox out of his bag, his eyes were bright, and he had a cheerful grin. Despite his concern about Jane, he was happier than I'd seen him in ages.

But what about Albert? Was he really sorry, or was he up to something?

Chapter 8

Englebert and Animal Control

Whenever we rounded the last corner into Quiller's Bend, I always scanned the hillside for Englebert. I liked seeing his familiar shape moving through the grass. Today we all searched for him anxiously. But there was only the shelter and water bucket. Had the Perkinses taken over already? Just how were they going to "get rid of him"?

"He's not there!" My stomach rolled.

"Who's not there?" Paula demanded. She hadn't understood a thing that had gone on lately.

"Englebert!" Davy stopped and stared. "Have they taken him away already?"

"No, I see him." Marty pointed. "Behind the oak tree. Look!"

I saw a movement, half-hidden by the leaves. But it wasn't only the black of Englebert's coat. There was something else. Something red.

When we got there, we found that the red thing was Jane's jacket. She was crouched beside Englebert, one arm draped around his neck. He was sitting down, chewing his cud, with his legs folded under himself. He swallowed. Then he turned his head, and rubbed one of his horns against her shoulder.

We could see she'd been crying, but she was calm now.

"H-He d-doesn't know," she whispered. She patted the bump between his horns, then stroked his ears.

We knew what she meant. Englebert thought this was the same as any other day. He expected me to have saved him something good from my lunch.

"B-But I w-won't l-let them!" The tears started again. With her spare hand, she felt for a stick that lay beside her in the long grass.

I could picture Englebert facing Richard and Mrs. Perkins. The goat's stiff legs would be set apart. He'd be slashing with his horns and snorting through his nostrils! Jane would be at his side, the stick raised above her head.

I sat down beside them and opened my bag. Englebert sniffed at my lunchbox. There was half an apple left. I held it while he took dainty bites. The boys stayed on the far side of the fence. Englebert still wouldn't let them come any closer.

I don't know how long Jane and I sat there stroking Englebert and feeding him handfuls of grass. It must have been a couple of hours, at least. The sun was almost down when Dad came to get us.

"It's dinnertime, Sharma. And your grandma wants you home," he said to Jane. He didn't often speak in such a quiet voice. He must have known Jane was upset.

She hugged the goat's neck tightly.

"Come on, Jane. It's late and they won't come for him tonight." I touched her arm. "He'll be all right till the morning." I took her hand and stood up. She must have believed me, because after a glance back at Sea View Road, she stood up, too.

I was stiff and cold from sitting on the wet grass. Jane didn't look any better. After Dad and I watched her walk slowly up the sidewalk and in through her own gate, he asked me what it was all about. So I told him. Right back from the day Mr. Quiller died.

"And now the Perkinses are going to get rid of Englebert, as well as bulldoze the house. He belonged to Mr. Quiller, and Jane loves him."

When we'd finished dinner, Dad said, "I won't be long." And he went out. When I went to bed, he still hadn't come back.

I was awake half the night worrying about Jane and Englebert, so I slept in. The next morning, I was running late. I ran down the path still eating my toast.

Marty, Jane, and Davy were waiting at the gate. As we passed Mr. Quiller's house, Jane stopped and looked back at Englebert. Then she grabbed my sleeve. "D-Does your d-dad always k-keep his promises?" she asked.

"What's she talking about?" I said to Marty.

"Don't you know?" he asked.

I shook my head.

"We don't know much about it, either," said Marty. "Your dad came over to talk to Grandma last night, but she sent us away to watch TV."

"Th-Then your d-dad c-c-c-c..." Jane was stuck. She couldn't finish what she was saying.

Marty took over. "He came in and promised Jane that he wouldn't let anyone take Englebert away."

"There you go, Jane," Davy said, patting her shoulder, "your precious Englebert is safe." Then he muttered, "But I don't know why you'd want him!"

"But there's something else," Marty went on. "Where are they going today at 2:30 p.m.?"

"Who?"

"Your dad and Grandma. When she opened the door to let him out, he said he'd meet her at 2:30 p.m."

I know Dad would have intended to keep his promise about Englebert, but he hadn't bargained on Mrs. Perkins. As we came into Quiller's Bend that afternoon, I saw the white car parked up on Sea View Road. In front of it was a dark blue van. I couldn't read the writing on it from this distance, but I knew what it was. It had bars over the back windows, and it belonged to the city pound. It had come to school one day to collect a stray dog that had been hanging around in the schoolyard. It didn't take a genius to guess what it was up there for!

As we raced through our gate, I saw Mrs. Perkins on the edge of the road. She had one hand holding her hat on to keep it from blowing away. With the other hand, she was pointing at Englebert. At this stage, he was quietly cropping some thistles. A man in a blue uniform was trying not to slip as he made his way down through the wet grass. He carried a stick in one hand and a net bunched up in the other. Richard slithered along beside him. As Jane and I climbed through the fence, I looked around for Albert. There was a shape in the white car, but I couldn't tell if it was him.

Englebert lifted his head. He'd seen us coming. He'd be thinking about what we had left over from lunch.

"Keep back, girls! He's dangerous!" the man called. If the man didn't keep his distance, he'd find out just how dangerous. We'd have to keep him away.

Englebert got as near to us as his chain would let him. The man kept coming. Sliding downhill, he was faster than we were climbing up. We still had five or six yards to go, when he stopped to sort out his net.

Jane's last few steps were jet propelled. She flung herself at Englebert and wrapped her arms around his neck. I scrambled up after her. "Who said he's dangerous?" I yelled. By this time, Englebert was taking little bites of my chocolate cookie.

"He's already attacked that woman's son," the man said as he pointed over to Mrs. Perkins. "Just get out of the way and let me catch him." Carrying the net above his head, he came closer.

"You'd better keep back," I warned. "He only likes girls!"

Now the man was inside the circle. Englebert took Jane by surprise. He pulled away and swung around to face the man. He shook his head. His beard whipped from side to side, and his chain rattled. He did a few trial stabs in the air with his horns and started to walk up the hill.

Jane launched herself onto the chain, which was dragging through the wet grass. Her weight slowed Englebert down, so when the man flung his net at the spot where he expected Englebert to be, it fell like a giant spiderweb onto the grass. Englebert marched across it, towing Jane behind him.

The man saw the goat coming, horns first, and he began to back away. Richard was scrambling up the hill, screaming, "Mommy! Mommy!"

I followed Englebert and Jane, holding a banana skin at arm's length. It was all I had that might tempt the goat to stop. And he did stop at last, but only because Jane had hooked his chain around an old tree stump. He snorted and glared until the man was standing beside his van again. Richard was still sobbing and hanging onto his mother.

Jane and I hugged Englebert while he chewed the last strip of banana skin. We shouldn't have laughed. We shouldn't even have smiled, but we couldn't help it.

"You're right, Mrs. Perkins," the man said. "He's a dangerous animal."

"And he's on our property!" She waved one hand toward the notice on the builder's shed.

Then Albert appeared. He had been waiting in the car. "He doesn't look too dangerous to me," he said. They all stared at us. Englebert was nuzzling Jane's neck while she stroked his ears.

"All the same, I want him off our land immediately," Mrs. Perkins insisted.

"But it's not ours yet," Albert said. "Dad was complaining this morning that the lawyer hadn't done anything about the agreement."

"Yes. Well. It will be ours! Why else did your father put his shed here?"

"It was because he had to move it from his last job and he had nowhere else to put it. Didn't you hear him tell us that on Saturday?"

The man from the pound gave up. "I'll come back when all this is sorted out," he said. "Now, if someone could just get me my net, I'll be off."

I was all for handing it over, but Jane was still afraid he'd use it to catch Englebert.

"He said he'd go when he got it!" I reasoned. But Jane didn't trust anyone. At least, not where Englebert was concerned.

It looked like a standoff. Englebert wouldn't let the man get his net, and we weren't going to give it to him. Then another car parked in front of the van. It was ours. Dad got out and opened the door for Grandma Lawson. She wore her navy blue coat with the fur collar and her hat with the daisies. They'd been somewhere important.

Mrs. Perkins demanded that Dad make me get the net so that the man could catch Englebert and remove him from her property. The man insisted that he didn't want to catch "that beast." All he wanted was to retrieve his net. Richard was still yelling that the goat was trying to get him.

Grandma Lawson had her back to everyone. She stood on the edge of the road, leaning on her cane and gazing out over Quiller's Bend. Dad waited patiently for a gap in the noise. When it came, he said, "Mrs. Perkins, this is not your property, so you might as well go home. And if you're worried about your husband's shed, he will be here within half an hour to remove it."

Then he came down the hill as far as the end of Englebert's chain. He crouched in the long grass. "Jane," he said. "Last night, I promised you no one would take Englebert away, and I meant it. He's quite safe." Then his mouth twisted up in a little grin. "But it's just as well you were here this afternoon. He'd have done a bit of damage with those horns if they'd gotten him into the van."

All the time Dad was talking, he kept glancing at Englebert, who was snorting at him and stamping one front foot. He still didn't like boys – or men. Not even when they were on his side.

"But what's going on, Dad?" I asked. I was confused about who owned what, and what Grandma Lawson had to do with it.

Dad stood up. "I'm taking Mrs. Lawson home now. I'll tell you all about it after dinner." He trudged back up the hill, helped Grandma Lawson into the car, and drove off. Mrs. Perkins and the man in the van had gone, too. The road was empty, except for Albert. This was the second time he'd been left behind.

Chapter 9

Mr. Quiller Lives On

There were three boys to move Englebert's shelter this time. Albert didn't wait to be invited. He just joined in the heaving and tugging. Afterward, we all sat on Davy's porch and ate popcorn that Mrs. McGregor had made for us.

"Why does your mother hate Englebert?" Davy asked Albert, as he tossed a handful of popcorn to Queenie. The rest of us had been wondering about that, but it took Davy to demand an answer.

"It's my fault, I guess. I told those lies about what happened that day, and she ended up looking silly."

"Why did you do it?"

"Because I couldn't think of anything else to get myself out of trouble." Albert was quiet for a moment. "But I've never done it again."

"Done what?"

"Told any lies."

We all stared at him. That didn't sound right.

"Not any big ones." He grinned as he spoke. We'd still have to watch him.

Then he went on, "And I was jealous of all of you. You were friends with each other, and I was left out. Anyway, Mom was always looking for a good story about the rough kids from Quiller's Bend."

I knew that last part was teasing, but Marty took him seriously. He'd often been on the wrong end of those stories, and he was still annoyed.

"She must be rotten!" he snapped.

"No, she's not. She just gets an idea into her head and it's hard to get it out. Besides, she's my mom." We went on chewing for a bit, then Albert said to Marty, "Anyway, did you get my letter?" His words came out through a mouthful of popcorn.

"Yep."

"Did Mr. Atwood say anything else?"

"Yep." Marty hadn't said much, but he'd calmed down. I knew he felt better about the whole thing.

And that was the end of it.

While Dad and I were doing the dishes that night, he told me his side of the story.

"I'd had enough of you kids being upset," he began, "and Jane appeared to be worse off than the rest of you. So I went to see Mrs. Lawson last night."

I nodded. That was no news.

"And she told me a surprising story. It appears that in Mr. Quiller's will, he left instructions that the house and land were to be sold and..." he hesitated, "and the money was to be kept in trust for Jane and Marty."

"Mr. Quiller left all his money to the twins?" I nearly dropped the plate!

"It's not a fortune," Dad said. "There's only the house and the land. I don't know what they're worth. Mrs. Lawson wasn't too clear about the whole thing, so I went with her to see Mr. Brannigan, the lawyer, this afternoon. It seems that one-third of the money can be used for things they need now. Clothes, new beds, new bikes, that sort of thing. And the rest is to be divided between the two of them and placed in a trust fund for their education. Mr. Quiller especially mentioned singing lessons for Jane."

Why them, and not Davy and me? He'd known us longer. Didn't he like us? I was jealous. It wasn't fair!

Then I thought about all the kids who picked on Jane because of her stutter. They picked on Marty a bit, too. But not if he could hear them. And I remembered all the times they stayed home helping their grandma while Davy and I went swimming or to the movies.

Yes. Mr. Quiller had been fair.

"So you see that when they got Mr. Perkins's offer, after it seemed no one wanted the property at all, the lawyer was eager to take it. But – there was a snag!"

"Do you mean Englebert?"

"Partly. Although Mrs. Lawson didn't know that at the time. It appears that those children keep a lot of things from their grandmother. They don't like to worry her. Actually, she hadn't told them about the will."

"So what else went wrong?"

"Have you ever looked really carefully at the old Quiller house?"

"Well, it is ancient and kind of spooky. I don't know if I'd want to live there." I remembered staring at the house the other day during the rainstorm.

"Yes, it is very old. And did you ever wonder why it's never been renovated inside – no new kitchen, or anything like that?"

I had wondered, then I'd just thought that Mr. Quiller liked it that way.

"It's because it's the oldest house in this part of the country, and because it was built in a special way," Dad went on. "So there's a preservation order on it."

"What does that mean?"

"It means that you can't tear it down, and you can't make any changes unless they're done in that same special way. It would cost a lot to fix it up, and Mr. Quiller didn't have the money."

"Can't tear it down" were the words running through my mind. "Can't tear it down!" And that's what Mr. Perkins was going to do. He'd planned to flatten it with the bulldozer!

"So Mr. Perkins won't want it after all?" I said as I put the last pot into the cupboard.

Dad shook his head. "That means the twins will just have to wait for their money until another buyer comes along."

"Someone that likes goats, I hope."

"We'll have to see. Anyway, Englebert's safe in the meantime."

As usual, the first thing I saw when I went upstairs to my bedroom that night was the display shelf with all the gaps. I still didn't feel good about it, although Mom had promised me extra money to buy some more. I think she felt bad about letting Richard have the run of the house.

And through the window on the opposite wall, I could see the Quiller house. It was solid and strong. It didn't matter who bought it, they'd never be allowed to pull it down. It would be there forever.

And so would Mr. Quiller!

From the Author

I spent my childhood in a place just like Quiller's Bend. And although that was sixty years ago, the same cluster of houses is still there, tucked into the hillside. I expect that another generation of children play together, argue, and take care of each other in just the way we did.

Of course, *The Kids from Quiller's Bend* is fiction, and the children are – for the most part – fictional characters. But I must admit that I did know a boy like Albert Perkins!

When grown-ups look back at their childhoods, they often remember only the good times, but I'll never forget the long, weary walk up that hill to home every day.

Marie Gibson

From the Illustrator

At the time I was illustrating this book, two of my children were almost the same age as the children from Quiller's Bend. So I felt I could identify with these characters and, hopefully, bring them to life.

I used my children, George, Alyssa, and Michael, as models, along with some of their friends. I discovered Hashika playing basketball, and she agreed to model for Sharma. Hashika's family modeled for the Menie family portrait.

Like the characters from Quiller's Bend, I grew up in the country, where we knew every tree and hill. We never owned a goat, but we did have a pet sheep named Sam, who was given run of the farm. I'm happy to say that my dad never considered Sam a member of the muttony masses, instead he was given the superior status of a family pet.

Linda McClelland

Written by **Marie Gibson**
Illustrated by **Linda McClelland**
Edited by **Frances Bacon**
Designed by **Kristie Rogers**

02 01 00 99 98 97
10 9 8 7 6 5 4 3 2 1

Distributed in the United States by
  Rigby
  a division of Reed Elsevier Inc.
  P.O. Box 797
  Crystal Lake, IL 60039-0797

Printed by Colorcraft, Hong Kong
ISBN: 0-7901-1698-7